SEX AT NOON TAXES

SALLY VAN DOREN

poems

SEX AT NOON TAXES

LOUISIANA
STATE
UNIVERSITY
PRESS

)|(

BATON
ROUGE

Published by Louisiana State University Press
Copyright © 2008 by Sally Van Doren
Manufactured in the United States of America

An LSU Press Paperback Original
FIRST PRINTING

DESIGNER: *Amanda McDonald Scallan*
TYPEFACE: *Whitman, Arcana GMM Std*
PRINTER AND BINDER: *Thomson-Shore, Inc.*

Library of Congress Cataloging-in-Publication Data
Van Doren, Sally.
  Sex at noon taxes : poems / Sally Van Doren
    p. cm.
  ISBN-13: 978-0-8071-3311-8 (pbk. : alk. paper)
  I. Title.
  PS3622.A58548S49 2008
  811'.6—dc22

                                        2007021775

The author gratefully acknowledges the editors of the following publications, in which some of
the poems herein appeared previously, some in slightly different form: *American Poet:* "Faithful to
Error" and "Hence My Transport"; *Barrow Street:* "Being Eaten"; *Columbia Poetry Review:* "Impa-
tient"; *Crayon:* "April," "Congenial," "Lunacy," "One Other Sign of Knowledge," "Pasture,""Praxis,"
and "Story"; *The Dead Horse Review:* "Sex at Noon Taxes"; *Delmar:* "Sited"; *Hamilton Stone Review:*
"Good Friday" (as "Friday"); *LIT:* "Conjunction" and "Preposition"; *Pool:* "Faithful to Error" and
"Lover"; *River Styx:* "The Secret"; *Snow Monkey:* "Would"; *2River View:* "Girlhood."

For Lorenzo
  Amor, che nel penser mio vive e regna

CONTENTS

I

SEX AT NOON TAXES

After a painting of the same title by Ed Ruscha

From the ghost town's
fencepost, my lariat ropes
your palindromic peak
and hauls it to our bedroom,
where the timbers arch to hold off
the mountain's hooves—no
avalanche turns snowfall into
uncorraled horseshoes.
The steeds bear us upslope.
We reach the muddy cleft
between Maroon Bells
and Crested Butte, gnawing
on caribou and warmed
liver of once noble clk.

PASTURE

Categorize a cough.
Catch a calf, laugh,
fart. Forget the phonics
of the focal/fecal. Phrase,

fashion, and effuse. Frigid
sapphirine captures the
fragment. We all, together,
web our fingers and paint,

upside down, caricatures.
Have enough. Carve out
one piece of the veal's heart.
Red wine can cauterize any

carton of haute couture.
May we lather the cast? Yes.

LOVER

Show me the color of heat.
Is it my quiver or yours?

How hot does red get?
When does white take cover?

I refine my sense of
pain when you touch me

with something blue. That
flame travels through my

airways now; can't you
stop talking? I never

want to hear your face
again—it melts what

madness I use as varnish;
tinting tongue, boiling word.

IMPATIENT

I want it to come
right away, like it
did last night, when
I didn't know what
I needed, when I
thought I was sick,
when I was fed up with
how much time it took
for salt to turn to water.

I will not name it
here, but if you part
your lips, I will relieve
you of your share
of our burden.

CASTLE

The sword's sheath
lies on the ottoman,
its blade on the floor
near the master bed.

Wrinkled sateen
drapes the cherry
frame built for a
king who rules with
sovereign complacence.

Look, no blood stains
the carpet under the
knife. Fealty
cowers, fastened
to goose feathers.

LUNACY

The moon woman argued
with the man in the womb.
*Does it behoove you to
watch the peony's bloom*

droop? The white worm
in the leather-leaf viburnum
huddled in the honeysuckle's
shade. Wild strawberries

grew in craters. Dust,
caught in micro-leit-
motif, leapt from
the garden into orbit.

Every day is yahrzeit.
We are the flying Perfect.

MOTHER TONGUE

Excerpt the choc-o-
late, lately, Italian,
French, the sunshine

of the postprandial,
wind, Queen Anne's lace
and the deck chair.

Sniff, giggle, scratch.
Comb the chalk bits
in the butterfly's route.

Light lights up the granular
and rubber croons in the hollow.
Residual paper muddies craft.

Along comes the sentence to
break up the monotony of possession.

WOULD

it be possible to write over the
sketch, the ink covering

first his drawing, then my
scribbles, Twombly-esque or

far from it, real words with
spelled meanings, caffeine-

generated pronunciations,
emotion served over a puree

of cocoa and egg yolk, vertical
lines carving ahead of time,

curlicues added after
the burst stamen, the golden

pistol, the implement, goddam-
mit, of the spirit?

SHOULD

My hobby, shoul-
dering this full-time.

The term's renewed.
Ought flows with gusto
and brags about its
macro-mood. Liquid
musts emit gas-vapors
and I drown in the
mist. What's over-
cast flogs me. Does
suction strap air
bubbles to mass?

Sleek cesium pools,
timing my living.

PARROT

Improvisation willed inquiry to abandon
the vernacular's Ozark debut; the untried blurred
the steward's request; more conjunctions reclined in cabins

soaked with floodwater. Sex calls the body
away from art. Red cyclists, yellow-centered, bit the glass roof,
the sound of the twin clattering on gravel. Green and terra-cotta mold

in unison, forcing, supporting and embodying
the sky's produce. Helmets and alyssum. The brain
protects livelihood stolen from a British book. Snow

on the screen, home,
fingernails, seat belts and
hot towels run to the end of the

preposition. Which el-
lipsis omits love?

ENVY

When speech accumulates
and the circumference
of the mindscape is threatened
by a worn valve, it is

time to make a gesture
of incantation, time to
warn the beasts who
wish to annex that

piece of the mind,
that hovering wilts
the pink flower, that
in missing the caveat,

we fortify our theorems,
and sleep through our dreams.

MENTOR

The you-ness of your
use or overuse of
the second person plural
exceeds discursive
hegemony. Reductive
theories swell with
the address, as all
of us are, now
that we know you,
swollen, not into
your balloon of yes,
but inflated past
our scripted histories.
Use us as you would.

BEING EATEN

Her aegis, crap really,
sat at the head of the table,
the monotype of the beaver
resting at an angle just behind
her worm arms. She served
turpentine with a dollop
of gesso, which we slurped
until the pastels smeared
down our chins. With
charcoal napkins pressed
to our lips, we aimed
for the ta and spit
into the center of the who.
Soup to tuba, ekphrastic.

GEPHYROPHOBIA

If there is a bridge,
I cannot see it,
but I know I want
to cross it, to walk
from one isthmus
of the self's fragment
to a peninsula,
a teat leaking
honey milk, sweet
libation from
the other side.
I am slack-mouthed
and breathing
through my nose.

PROPOSITION

Let's say your left breast
Is much larger than your right,
And you are not a fine-tuned
Distortion of a woman as
John Currin makes you out to be,
But you sag as you age.
Why wear the lambswool
Sweater anymore?
                    The aureole
Puckers under lip's breath like
A sea anemone's spores open.
You can still be wet paint.
Your canvas is the ocean.
Sprout gills and watch your nipples
Float like masts in the salted air.

II

PREPOSITION

The before took us right up to
the after, even though under
meant we should not try over,
from being stronger than to,

up shying from its ascent
in the face of down. I held
on to you and beside you
I became with and about.

In our around, the near/far
could turn away and toward,
within the without. By my above
and your below, the wheres and

whens retreated, leaving time
and space stranded, in off, on out.

CONJUNCTION

Furthermore, until but
dethrones however
while nevertheless pilots
since out of that's

stratosphere and or
submits to nor,
therefore reigns,

except when nonetheless
has yet to champion
neither and then
predeceases if,

on the one occasion
because does not
respond to either.

PRONOUN/PUNCTUATION

He who parsed us left us with a floating
colon, an ellipsis enjambed by a full-stop.

We had paced with a question
taped to our backs; in post-op

it slimmed to an exclamation point.
Commas shadow us; brackets enclose

our parentheses. See the slash
in this title? I have left her out and you.

She erases the hyphen, and all of you,
condensed in apostrophes, blow your

quotation marks into my dreams.
Their asterisks crowd my lexicon:

relatives, possessives and personals. I do hear
them calling; they are not saying nothing.

HENCE MY TRANSPORT

Will it be a lift,
        the moment of individuation,

or a lilt? One tithes. The other
        has left life and me

to wonder whether filth tilts
        mind's balance, heart

being lithe now, with the felt title
        of mother, father having

fallen out of the file. A fell self
        flits in this fall-lit afternoon.

Give me a full year, not a filet,
        till I unfill myself, awful,

a foal fed too often
        on if/then's ethyl.

SITED

He was here then, back
when I was there; you
were with me; you weren't,

the then being before the
beginning of the unlife,
the not-thereness having
not yet taken hold of his

hand. The trust in his
estate was in its undoing,
the disassembled vehicle
of non-necessariness.

Many mounds of here
landed on his whereness;
we hoard them.

BREATHE WHEN I EXPIRE

the here is the why of summer this sentimental hole wedged
between Paris Provence and a labored wedding

removed from the when of death and rain the where of a scream and a white face
the how of the gash the blue bone and the fall into the pillow

the other coming the smush of the younger heart to the yellow her the whelping
over how to watch

as with the other fully knowing only what to wear the older went and won't
appear

the whether has no bearing on the when of now or the necessity of the end of
August

hike to the pool and hear the gush ride the river with nothing the color of daylight
is orange the rock red the walls of green close

what horse would rear here now that time favors a dry valley and torture tires of
the current

BLUE RONDO

Everything is permanent.
          temporary.
          transitive.
          intransitive.

The use of active transitive verbs is preferable.
The verb to be is weak.
A metaphor is a house without a mother.
To be strong, it is necessary not to link one thing to another via transition.

Corollaries are constructs of being.
At one time, adverbs were emblems of codependency.
Is is at once what was was.
Passive and past have been sisters to has-beens.

Having been a was, am is now a conjugate without a colon;
the clause's complexity is in question.

PRIMUR

Bedder not tew admit that
the auther of the pome, whos
vois has not bin perjered,
whos breth vybrates with

the phan's roteytion, whos
narrashun may bee unreliabl,
hs mor to say than the vegeteble
berger sizzling ovur charcoles,

kreates altitoodes fromb which
to plummit fertively, sincs into
plush orange pyle, then sirfases
too inform thoes wating that

the oke leef shaches, that won
centence is not the biginning.

ONE OTHER SIGN OF KNOWLEDGE

The *non*, the *anti*, and the *un*
are not antonyms of oxymorons,

negations of positive polar opposites
or, are they? How to say *yes*

to a flattened undeath,
a specific sifted unlife?

When unlove enters,
a lull halts

the fleet-of-binary-foot.
Hop from up to down.

Let the fit fight the ever-named,
the pronounced *no*, the particular

particularity of the answer
unmodified.

SOUTHERN GHAZAL-SONNET

Here, where the liminal tongue
    muscles out from the marital sheets;

here, where the key fits in the lock
    but does not open the door;

here, where the blades in the ceiling
    interrupt the light's source;

here, where imagined purposefulness
    combats resistance;

this, Sarah Frances, is the place you left
    home to get locked out from.

Your belongings are trapped under
    Dade County pine. Pry up

the floorboards to discharge
    your fantasies.

REVISITATION: KEY WEST CEMETERY

As the dollar bills peeled away
I sat on the edge of a tombstone
and counted the taboos in front of me:
necrophilia, incest and the listing of assets.

I smelled the stock price rise and fall
and imagined myself to be a pebble
in the path of the Cadillac slowly spreading
exhaust into the air which blessed my face

and the sun which warmed my cold eyebrows
and my invisible mustache. A turquoise
poinsettia grew in a cracked vase hiding
a granite America behind a plastic blade.

Such arrangements were made for us, dandelions
and carnations, bred by nature and by force.

TO SPEAK OF

The periscope navigates
the vaginal canal. Our lunar
eyes descend upon polyps.
Moon-tipsy, we step over
craters, walking on our hands.
My thumb outstretched tickles
the end of your cervix.
A wave pulls at my feet
and I squiggle out backwards,
my heels sponges imprinting
themselves on the urethra's
cavity. Will you urinate now
or do you ovulate instead
sending me the one tufted egg?

MARRIAGE

The name I use shuns none but
those doused in sentimental phlegm.
I peed in the spot where the frigate
pelicans nest. The *National Geographic,*

read in Worcester, wets the mouth
of the octopus from Kirkwood, Mo.
The he, him, other, far, far from the fart-
splattered walls of a Cornell box.

Will the sea stay on the jetty's edge?
Chicken fat foam unskimmed.
Salt, butter, sugar and alcohol.

The engine of sex crowds the sky. Land
dances under the mattress pad. Call me and
I will answer. Watch me map the periplum.

EXCURSION

The cellophane facial
answered the telephone
like a cracker stacked
in wax paper. The surfeit
whore stole her share
of the absorbent shore.

Where were we supposed
to surface, hoarse from
sharin' the storm with
the superficial? We straddled
the storefront, shed our T-shirts,
and shod ourselves in purple
flip-flops. Shoes reassured
us, the meter of the feet.

TO THE BIGHT

Here, you can get up before breakfast, salt pressing
    into your pores, unsure of cloud cover, reticent sun,

make sandal steps past the electric substation, charged,
    hungry for buckets of dead fish. Out on the pier,

Lucia, Double-Decker, Boom-Boom and *Sharon Lee*
    bobble in Sunday's wake. The minister has not

yet taken up the pulpit. A lacquered mast rises
    with its twin and the King Conch burrows deeper under the dock.

There is an excursion you must take. You load your
    pockets with coins, pulp and splinters

and buy a pilgrim's ticket. The ferry harbors
    holds and holds of ones like you, cars, bikes,

mopeds. The buffering ficus and palm fronds
    desist; you are out to sea.

III

TO BECOME WORLD

In the beginning the girl
told her story, although
each time her words fell
through her legs, a stain

wet her underpants. It was
uncomfortable, this
intimacy between her two
mouths, breeding her tongue's

distaste for common speech.
With a pair of tweezers, she
plucked out every pubic hair

and affixed them to her chin.
She stroked her beard
when she spoke and listened.

GIRLHOOD

Alone in the basement
hiding naked behind
the washing machine,
I spied on my father
looking for his ironed
shirt, watched two
repairmen work on the
furnace and heard
another flush out the
drains.
      Girl, soundless,
pinned between the hot-
water hookup and the
AC adaptor on an ever-
lasting winter morning.

SEVENTEEN

I am sorry that I did not have sex with you,
even though you wanted to, and, looking back,

I see that you needed to, and your complaint
that we always made out with our clothes on,

while it shamed me, underscored that
we had not bared our flesh to one another,

and when you sat beside me at the reunion dinner,
we kissed, but I did not get to say, thank you;

that those clothed moments, on the grass,
against the tree, in that garage, opened me,

and though I still would not sleep with you
now, last night I dreamt you were lying

naked next to me, and I touched you,
before my husband drove you from our bed.

THE SECRET

We drove to Lesterville.
His flesh smelled like onions
and when he pressed on
the gas, I pressed my hand
on his thigh, his stone-
washed jeans warm under
my fingers. Our sweat
pores opened and leaked
out over those hot vinyl
seats. We swam in that
sweet liquid, churning
in our carwash, rinsing
in the water we became at the edge
of the lake we finally reached.

PERSONA AVERSION

How to slip out
and access the Hyde
in me? Jekyll and Mom
off at the cotillion, the crino-
lines skating down the run-
way to the Khorassan.
Bowing deep to the veiled
prophet, the escorted
skirt the abscess, each kid
leather glove embalming
its girl from fingertip to
biceps. The ad-libs dance,
words pumping double-time
through reinforced toes.

CONTRARY

For women some of who they are
is what they wear and how
they wear their hair that day.

It's rare to get past the flip
of the tress and the gloss
of the puckered lip.

Who can eat lunch when
Vanity thrusts herself out
from every perfumed spore?

Swallow surfeit's opposite
this once, and smell Beauty
moving up from under woman's
widening hips, an extra serving
on the plate of the starved aesthete.

YULETIDE

We shall choose a stoic font
this time and hang it from the branch
of the Christmas tree which imprints
Season's Greetings on the ice cubes
in the scotch tumblers dousing
the throats of the CEOs done
with a week's worth of weak
revenues; good wives rarely

crack when mistletoe whizzes by
and ordinary language dissolves,
the hostess' breath filling
her emptied house, the last
party favor passed out,
the *Happy* affixed to *Holiday.*

HEARTH FIST

The knuckle of the house
Was flustered. Soot spread
Into its creases, blighting
The thumb's pad. The concentric

Ovoids, which once confirmed
Its spiraling identity, flapped
Against the clapboards,
The shutters loosening from their

Pegs. Shovel, blow poke and
Colonial tongs blackened
Under the smoke's panicked
Flood up the stone chimney.

Flames ironed the house's hand
And like kindling, it crackled and split.

OASIS

The overactive mind can blame the hummingbirds
      or the bees which hover in and

around the chuparosa mining the red tubes
      for midwinter sustenance.

The sanatorium succeeds
      with blue skies and lucid air,

the roots of the Smoke Tree finding
      water deep below the desert wash.

Breath produces oleander and
      bougainvillea, and any encounter

with a cactus is just that; pluck out
      the offending needle and

continue. This is the time for succulents
      and fan palms; take to the transplant.

APRIL

I chart the psyche,
observing how I
force myself to speak
to you, imagining that
together we might
transform a life.

Why this need
to document change,
to reverse a mood,
to carry forward the time
when magnolias bloom?

Let's follow the itinerant we
up and over the jonquil's back,
treading on its spilled bullion.

GOOD FRIDAY

In quest of a question
Caroline carved lines
in her back, beckoning
reflective responses
flecked with vespers,
the sponges of the sage,
jeopardizing only the only,
the pejorative dope-
pushers, supine, rushing
to kept tactics, pet
kittens caught in nets
meant for fish. Amen.
Soffits high and low
hid the owl's gift.

EASTER

Hyacinths come first

    here, forsythia close

        behind. Jonquils and

daffodils sprouting

    up before we are ready

        to receive the light of

April. The oaks' leaves

    don't yet give us cover

        and the sheared air

            sears the cornea.

Could we hide

    in the azalea bud?

        Lilies wake us. We're

            singing purple.

DISCOURSE

Portions of variables exfoliate.
Speech mimics restless quarters;
stresses, buried, infraredless, sprout
toward the phrase, which extends itself
to clarify action. Sounds of nonsense,
armrests, trunks, the birch by the Truckee,
on its back, with a female pinned, convex,

wet, then dry, pinked by light, pruned
for recitation. Prose ties the Aspen roots
to the geography of four weeks.
As if assertions could.
The lovely pussy doesn't dactyl.
E's infinity needs space. In the dream he
was at the party, healthy, wearing a coat and tie.

EQUINOX

Did it know in the September refraction
through the plate glass (the house faced
west, wall-sized windows sun-troughs
through brick) the man in the green wool blazer
whose bald head reared before the pine tree,
blocking the acuity of the retreating summer-minus?

How to measure the space between
the bed three nights ago and a car pulling
in the driveway? And what did Time sound like?
It was iambic, a rising beat hidden in the trope,
turning at the sight of him. Someone had given
permission to isolate them from the closure of a day.

Breeze came, and, like skin, peeled,
leaving new layers, falling to fall.

HETEROGRAPH

The yes is unpoached, untamed.
  The fiddle plays while

the bluegreen sky falls. The shine
  of it. Sniff up into it.

What groans, what stalls?
  The beat runs. Pressure.

Clutter. Cunning under one
  eyelid. This valve

opens. This air wilds
  the dropping, the particles.

What of the gesture? Reticent.
  Repellent. Receptive.

Running from it. Running
  toward it.

IV

FAITHFUL TO ERROR

Every virtue in excess is a defect.
—CHARLES VAN DOREN

I once read
Poem No and
my first face
aspired to
hamper its
choir by
cutting through
the querulous
funnel web rustling
around its neck;
Poem Yes hung from
one of those split
threads and as it swung
I swatted at its potential.

CONGENIAL

I digress
from the ru-
minative;
memory
replaces
fiction; talk
covers what
the is was.
The cumu-
lativeness
of a cloud—
when did it
cross the hay
moon's sky?

PRAXIS

For Jackson Moore

What segues when you're
waiting in the shaft,
avoiding transgressive
skewers, idioms
which novice buck
moons swallow
whole?
       Waiting for the
answer to when and
the rebuttal to why.
Speaking the language
of the strawberry.
Stuttering buds
with lilies and hostas.

RECORD

Tell me what it is to know nostalgia,
To recognize the face which appears
In the raspberry patch and calls to me
Twenty years later, reminding me that
A was the one who asked me to a movie,
That B took me sailing, that C slid
His hand under my criss-crossed bra,
That D offered me a drive through
France in her parents' BMW, that E
Broke my hymen with his thumb, that
F plied me with tequila, that G rolled
Me on a nest of sticks. I'll tell
You my secrets in return and we'll
Forget them, together, with every X and O.

CONNECTICUT SONNET

The paper made my eyes hurt
from the light in the sky which
cut through twelve days of rain
and fog and low pressure systems

which gave me headaches at breakfast
when I never get them and before
I could yell at the kids I realized
that it was weather, nothing else,

which was setting me off and
I tried to stay quiet and wait
for the clouds to empty themselves

on the already mildewed flax
and the strips of grass plastered
underneath the mower.

ODALISQUE

At 11:30, I took off what clothes I had on
except for my underwear and sports bra
and I crossed my left leg over my right so that
I would see five red toenails in descending order of size,

and I heard the tractor's motor charging up the hill
and I turned to see if it was coming behind my barn and
it was and I jumped up to grab my shirt which I had left
on the table and then I decided, no, that I was as covered

as if I had been wearing a bikini, and that Joseph was going
to park the tractor down there and that I had planned
to expose my body to the sun at this time, and then,

the tractor turned, the bucket scraping on a rock as it
headed toward Uncle Johnnie's field, and my skin
became sticky and all I heard were wind chimes.

REIFICATION

Carry me forward where the whippoorwill's
shrill bleats in late afternoon and
the darkening evening, where it pierces
the cloud tent, shooting out above fir tips
and lightning rods; for now I'm under
the cellar door, latched with a rusted bolt,
skirting puddles from recent rains, dodging
Colonial crossbeams frosted with
spiderwebs. Carry me up, carry me
sideways, carry me over that slot between
floorboards, away from the peeling
soggy plaster. I am a house,
whole, uninterrupted; drop me
on my foundation; hold me.

STORY

One shoe wants you.
It's distracting. Squint
to locate the scrap

of hypergraphia
waiting in the base
of the flugelhorn.

Once you forgot
syncopation and
an enemy stomped
on your bigamist

poetics. Convert
to anomaly. Purge
l=a=n=g=u=a=g=e,
purse and narrate.

PRESENTLY

we will pierce the hum
of mediocrity and
claw our way up its
backbone, digit by digit,
to hyperology's realm.

Here, we'll hallucinate
that our hemisphere
is the icon of the missing
Prime Meridian.

How to pinpoint
an equator when
the day's aspect
circumnavigates
an empty whole?

OBLIGATION

What extravagant
commodity is sex?
If I loan you principle,
will you pay me interest?

I take a lien on you and lick
the sweat under your armpits,
betting leverage will
establish credit. Your

mortgage sallies forth;
I redeem it with coupons.
Equity builds and we stay
invested, screwing till we're

past due. What do I owe
you once I've paid you?

WIG

I was excited at the
thought of becoming

someone else, a
reprieve from the

insistent I I was
before. I must admit

I had no idea I was
an actress, not a poet.

Relief and many sheets
of paper join September

leaves lying on, now
flying off, the driveway.

How is it fall never fails
to kill the green things?

POTION

What bland stimulant
bloats my prefrontal cortex,
tricking me into thinking
tension deserves attention?
I'll check the index.
Cocoon equals paradise.
In this glossary it's spelled
gambol. Take a chance
when you swig and swab.
Lubricate, stretch.
Usurp the butterfly's domain.
I'm not only the female
I wanted to be. I am
winged masculinity.

IMPEDIMENT

We had braced ourselves
For a collision with the tip
Of the undersea mountain,
But the nose of our
Submarine drove instead
Into the rooted tendrils
Of a mangrove swamp.

We opened the hatch
In the intertidal zone
Where we disembarked
Riding our skiffs over
Salt marshes, dead-ending
Our despairs into
Fine-silted sand dunes.

I LOVE DEPRESSIVES

They find me—in my dorm
room with razor blade and pills
trembling wanting to perform—
sisters teachers lusting eating
sweating sleeping leapers feasters
on morose morsels. They feed
not on my hostess flesh but
filaments of fervor and fear.

My guest list's incomplete. Come
drink yourself to death with me.
My nectar lures the weak the strong
the dispossessed. Laugh when I
catch you in my silo. That's my
anti-dote. I'll grind you to a chuckle.